# BOMB SQUAD TECHNICIAN:
## 12 THINGS TO KNOW

by Samantha S. Bell

STORY LIBRARY

MORE TO EXPLORE

**www.12StoryLibrary.com**

12-Story Library is an imprint of Bookstaves.

Developed and produced for 12-Story Library by Focus Strategic Communications Inc.

**Library of Congress Cataloging-in-Publication Data**
Names: Bell, Samantha, author.
Title: Bomb squad technician : 12 things to know / by Samantha S. Bell.
Description: Mankato, Minnesota : 12-Story Library, [2022] | Series: Daring and dangerous jobs |
Includes bibliographical references and index. | Audience: Ages 10–13 | Audience: Grades 4–6
Identifiers: LCCN 2020018553 (print) | LCCN 2020018554 (ebook) | ISBN 9781632359384 (library binding) |
ISBN 9781632359735 (paperback) | ISBN 9781645821038 (pdf)
Subjects: LCSH: Bomb squads—Juvenile literature. | Ordnance disposal units—Juvenile literature.
Classification: LCC HV8080.B65 B45 2022 (print) | LCC HV8080.B65 (ebook) | DDC 363.325/16—dc23
LC record available at https://lccn.loc.gov/2020018553
LC ebook record available at https://lccn.loc.gov/2020018554

Photographs ©: U.S. Department of Defense/E.J. Hersom, cover, 1; Bill Greenblatt/UPI/Alamy, 4; Image Vault/Alamy, 5; Alain Le Garsmeur "The Troubles" Archive/Alamy, 6; Ksp0704/CC3.0, 7; MoiraM/Alamy, 7; PJF Military Collection/Alamy, 8; U.S. Navy/Joshua, 9; PJF Military Collection/Alamy, 9; Militarist/Shutterstock.com, 10; AB Forces News Collection/Alamy, 11; Tero Vesalainen/Shutterstock.com, 11; Mode Images/Alamy, 12; Michael Matthew – Police Images/Alamy, 12; U.S. Marine Corps, 13; sandyman/Shutterstock.com, 13; ZUMA Press, Inc./Alamy, 14; Craig Steven Thrasher/Alamy, 15; Monika Wisniewska/Shutterstock.com, 15; Alexander Oganezov/Shutterstock.com, 16; 10News WTSP/YouTube.com, 17; agefotostock/Alamy, 17; PJF Military Collection/Alamy, 18; PJF Military Collection/Alamy, 19; Joaquin Ossorio Castillo/Shutterstock.com, 19; MilanTomazin/Shutterstock.com, 20; viper-zero/Shutterstock.com, 20; Gorodenkoff/Shutterstock.com, 21; Brad Vest/The Commercial Appeal/ZUMA Press/Alamy, 21; U.S. Air Force Photo/Alamy, 22; AB Forces News Collection/Alamy, 23; Eric Glenn/Shutterstock.com, 24; rCarner/Shutterstock.com, 25; Dumitrescu Ciprian-Florin/Shutterstock.com, 25; Bruce Stanfield/Shutterstock.com, 26; Sunshine Pics/Alamy, 27; sirtravelalot/Shutterstock.com, 27; Linda Kennedy/Alamy, 28; Pixel-Shot/Shutterstock.com, 29; Michael Candelori/Shutterstock.com, 29

## About the Cover

Bomb squad technician "neutralizing" a bomb.

Access free, up-to-date content on this topic plus a full digital version of this book. Scan the QR code on page 31 or use your school's login at 12StoryLibrary.com.

# Table of Contents

# Technicians Need Special Training

Bomb squad techs must wear protective body armor.

Many bomb technicians begin as police officers. Then they complete a program at a special facility. They study in the classroom. They also practice in real-life settings. That way, they will be able to use their skills in the real world.

Trainees learn about bomb disposal. They learn how to protect themselves. They study

## RAVENS CHALLENGE

Ravens Challenge training.

Each year, bomb experts participate in Ravens Challenge. They come from around the world. The challenge features many realistic bomb situations. Military and public safety technicians must work as teams. Together they develop plans and respond to the situations.

electronics and X-rays. They practice controlling robots to take bombs apart safely. They learn how to figure out whether a package is really a bomb.

Bomb experts must pass a test before they begin working. Then they continue to take courses and train. They know that bomb threats will become more advanced. They want to be ready.

# 3
**Years until technicians need to take the test again**

- All bomb experts receive the same kind of training.
- They learn to handle bombs in the same way.
- If more experts have to be called in, they can easily work together.

# Bomb Technicians Use Robots

When possible, bomb squad technicians use robots. The robots move and defuse bombs. The bomb squad controls the robots from a safe distance. That way, people aren't in danger.

Bomb disposal robots have been used since 1972. One of the earliest robots was called the Wheelbarrow Mark 1. It was an electric wheelbarrow with a claw. It could move car bombs. Today, the robots are remote controlled.

The robots have a lot of different tools. Cameras let the bomb squad see what the

Bomb robots save lives.

robot sees. They can look at the bomb from far away. The robot's claw acts as a hand. Some robots also have a saw for cutting. Some have special lights so they can work at night.

## THINK ABOUT IT

If you could build a robot, what would it do?

## 65

**Weight in pounds (29 kg) the F6A robot can lift**

- The F6A robot is one of the most useful robots.
- It can go across all kinds of surfaces. It can even climb stairs.
- It has an arm that can lift and move objects. It can drag an injured person to safety.

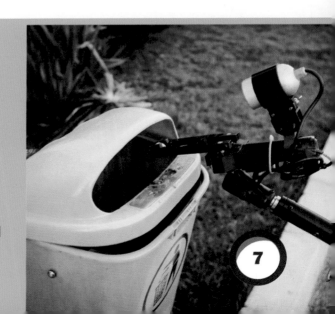

# EOD Technicians Are the Bomb Squad of the Military

Every branch of the military has a special bomb disposal unit. It is called the Explosive Ordnance Disposal (EOD) unit. The EOD units are experts on all types of bombs. They find and dispose of explosive weapons all over the world. They destroy hazardous ammunition. They get rid of outdated explosives. They protect other members of the military.

EOD techs must wear heavy, hot bomb suits.

EOD techs have to defuse explosives under water.

New EOD members go through months of training. The training is physically and mentally difficult. Trainees study the different types of bombs. They learn how to diffuse them. They do hands-on practice drills to make sure they're prepared. Some trainees don't make it through the program.

# 51

**Number of weeks of training time for new Navy EOD technicians**

- EOD units are always training and learning.
- They want to stay ahead in regard to bomb technology.
- Military training takes longer than other training. They are training for the battlefield.

## HELPING THE COMMUNITY

EOD units also work with regular citizens. Sometimes a community needs extra help with an explosive. For example, a person may find old ammunition from a war. Sometimes a bomb comes up on an old bombing range. The EOD units are ready to help.

# TRIPwire Is a Resource for All Bomb Squads

Improvised Explosive Devices (IEDs) are homemade bombs. They are used by people such as criminals and terrorists. IEDs come in many different forms. Some cause a small amount of damage. Larger ones can kill people. IEDs are made from everyday objects. An IED might be in a package or a backpack.

It could be in a car. Someone might be carrying it.

Emergency workers need as much information about IEDs as possible. To help with this, the Department of Homeland Security created a website called TRIPwire. It gives safety workers a way to share information. TRIPwire users include bomb squad

Every suspicious package gets the attention of the bomb squad.

members. It includes police officers and firefighters. It includes government officials and members of the military. TRIPwire provides these workers with the latest information about IEDs. This helps them prevent and respond to IED threats.

# 131
**Number of IED explosions in the US in 2018**

- TRIPwire is free for safety workers to use.
- They can find up-to-date documents, photos, and videos on the site.
- TRIPwire also provides information for the community about how to be prepared.

# Technicians Need Special Equipment

Bomb squads wear special suits for safety. The suits are made of Kevlar, a strong material that can take a lot of heat. They protect the squad members from fire and heat. Protective plates are in the front of the suits. These help shield techs against high-speed bomb pieces.

One of a technician's most important tools is a portable X-ray device. It takes X-ray images of suspicious packages and devices.

The images are displayed on a laptop. The bomb squad can see what's inside.

Explosives are safely transported in a special container. The container is so strong that if a bomb blows up, the blast will stay inside it. Bomb squads use it to take the explosives to a faraway location. Then they can inspect the bomb or detonate it.

## THINK ABOUT IT

Can you think of another time an X-ray machine might be used?

# 90

## Approximate weight in pounds (41 kg) of a bomb suit

- Bomb squad members don't wear gloves. They need to be able to use their hands easily.
- The helmet has a defogger and lights. It also has a ventilation fan.
- Some helmets have a built-in intercom system. That way, team members can communicate with each other.

**13**

# Bomb Technician Teams Are All Different

Not every bomb squad is the same. The makeup of the team depends on the city where it's located. Teams may consist of police officers, firefighters, or government agents. They can also be a combination of these.

Some squad members work full-time. When they aren't on a call, they spend their

Some local sheriffs' departments have bomb squads.

time training. In areas with smaller populations, most bomb squad positions are part-time. They have to keep up with their other duties, too. They also have to continue to train. Some bomb squads have both full-time and part-time team members.

## 28
### Number of full-time bomb squad members in Los Angeles

- The bomb squad responds to all calls about explosives.
- They respond to more than 1,000 calls each year.
- A team is always ready to go.

## FOUR-LEGGED MEMBERS

Many bomb squad teams also include canine units. These are made up of dogs and their handlers. The canine units often work under the direction of the police or sheriff's department. The dogs are trained to find explosives by sniffing. They can detect the chemicals used in explosives. Some dogs can even detect bombs carried by people.

**15**

# IABTI Brings Technicians Together

The public is always fascinated by bomb robots.

The International Association of Bomb Technicians and Investigators (IABTI) is an organization for bomb squad members. The group believes that bomb squads can do more when they work together. To help its members, IABTI provides training on explosive devices. It also keeps up with new equipment and laws.

IABTI also sponsors conferences. The conferences are held each year. Members can attend the conferences. They learn the latest information and techniques. They listen to special speakers and instructors. They also share information with each other. They build strong relationships.

The organization gives back to the community, too. A member named David Hyche had a blind daughter. He wanted her to

be able to participate in an Easter egg hunt. In 2005, he created a beeping Easter egg she could hear. Soon, more blind children were using the eggs. IABTI bomb squad members joined in. They put together the eggs used in the hunts. Today, IABTI sends beeping Easter eggs to any group that needs them.

# 5,000
## Number of members in IABTI

- IABTI was founded in 1974.
- It began in Sacramento, California.
- Bomb squad members from approximately 72 countries are involved.

# The FBI Trains Public Safety Technicians

The FBI Hazardous Devices School is a training site in Alabama. Technicians go there to learn to handle bombs. The school opened in 1971. It's the only school in the US that trains public safety bomb workers.

Students learn to handle bomb situations. They learn about different types of bombs, fuses, and electricity. They practice walking in heavy bomb suits. They learn how to steer robots through buildings.

The FBI trains explosive ordnance disposal (EOD) technicians.

It is tricky business to move a bomb in a safe.

The students have to pass psychological tests. They have to pass fitness tests, too. The school also conducts realistic bomb drills. That way, the students will be prepared for an actual bomb.

# 6

**Weeks of training time required at the Hazardous Devices School**

- The school covers 455 acres (184 ha).
- It includes 18 fake villages. These have churches and malls. They have schools and movie theaters.
- Students practice dealing with bomb threats in the villages.

Vietnam War Memorial in Washington, DC.

## AIDING THE TROOPS

The US was involved in the Vietnam War from 1965 until 1973. Many explosives were used in the war. The Hazardous Devices School opened during the Vietnam War. It was a way to help US troops prevent injuries from enemy explosives.

# Sometimes Technicians Detonate Bombs

Technicians work to make sure the bomb doesn't go off and hurt people. First, they try to make it safe to take apart. That way, they can use it as evidence. It may have the fingerprints of the person who made it.

But sometimes they have to detonate it. One way is to set off a small explosion, or disruption. A disrupter is anything that sets off the explosion. Sometimes the disrupter opens a bomb. Then the squad can see what's inside. Other times it cuts the fusing system.

A plastic water bottle makes a good disrupter. Bomb experts pack explosives in a straw in the center. Then they add

Sometimes it is necessary to blow up the explosive device.

Techs need to be certain which wire to cut when defusing a bomb.

a detonator. They set it next to the bomb. When it explodes, the pressure of the water inside the bottle tears apart the bomb's casing. It also cuts the bomb's connections before it explodes.

## 58

**Number of times the Memphis Police Department Bomb Squad was called out in 2018**

- A police officer goes out first to understand the situation.
- Then the bomb squad clears the area so no one gets hurt.
- The device is detonated in a special container.

Memphis police love their dogs.

# Women Can Be Bomb Technicians, Too

Air Force bomb disposal tech prepares a remote controlled vehicle.

Women also serve on bomb squads, including in the armed forces. They work alongside the men. They deal with the same emergencies.

But the job is very physically demanding. The heavy bomb suits weigh a lot. So do the explosives. Only about 10 to 20 of the 2,000 bomb technicians in the US are women.

But some who join the bomb squads are making history. In 2000, Officer Jody Gain

## FIRSTS FOR WOMEN

In 1974, Linda (Cranford) Cox overcame discrimination. She became the military's first female bomb squad member. She was also the first to lead her own bomb squad unit. She was the first to go to war. She was the first to receive the Bronze Star.

became the first female bomb squad member in Philadelphia, Pennsylvania. In 2018, Officer Melissa Aubrey became the first one in Charleston, South Carolina.

Bomb disposal is a career choice for female marines and others.

# 11.1
**Time in minutes of Lieutenant Ashley Sorenson's record**

- Lieutenant Sorenson was a bomb technician in the US Army.
- In September 2013, she ran a mile in a 75-pound (34 kg) bomb disposal suit.
- It was the fastest time for a female. The Guinness Book of World Records recorded her time.

# Bomb Technicians Can Earn Extra Money

Danger and long hours are part of a bomb technician's job.

Many bomb squad members start out as police officers. They earn the same amount as the other officers do. On average, bomb squad members usually earn $50,000 to $60,000 a year. But depending on their positions, they could earn more.

Bomb squad members are on call 24 hours a day. This means they may have to go to work any time of the day or night. They may earn extra for the unusual hours and dangerous work.

In the military, a technician's salary is usually based on their rank and the time spent in the

service. A starting yearly salary will be approximately $28,000. The military also offers help with college expenses. For example, qualified students in the Army can earn scholarships. These pay for the costs of college plus extra expenses.

**THINK ABOUT IT**

Would you like a job where you were on call? Why or why not?

Bomb technicians have to be prepared to work on short notice.

# $375
## Amount of extra money Army bomb technicians receive each month

- The military gives bomb experts extra pay because of their difficult job.
- They also gain experience for when they leave the service.
- They can use their skills in government service or law enforcement.

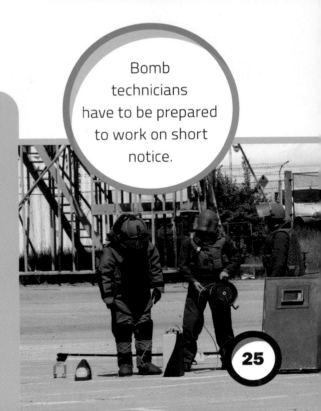

# BMAP Gets People Involved

A pipe bomb is fairly easy to make and can be very destructive.

The Office of Bombing Prevention (OBP) is part of the Department of Homeland Security. It was created because of terrorist events. The OBP works to prevent bombings within the US. It also tries to respond to them quickly. One way it does this is with the Bomb-Making Materials Awareness Program (BMAP).

BMAP is a program that provides people with information about improvised explosive devices (IEDs). Then people can be alert to possible dangers. For example, people can learn about the materials

Technicians need training to spot homemade bombs and then defuse them.

used to make bombs. That way, they'll be more likely to notice if someone buys those materials. They can watch for strange-looking devices. They can also look for suspicious behaviors.

In June 2019, a moving company was taking items from a house. One of the movers found something strange on a shelf. It was an IED. In January 2020, a man found an IED near his fence. Both times, bomb squads took care of the IEDs. No one was hurt by the bombs.

BMAP trains store employees to notice suspicious behavior.

# 1 hour

**Length of time for a BMAP course for store clerks**

- The workers can see what people are buying.
- The course shows them how to identify suspicious behavior.
- They also learn how to report it.

27

# More Daring and Dangerous Jobs

## Air Marshal

Government air marshals work on airplanes. They help keep the crew and passengers safe. Air marshals protect them from dangerous passengers or terrorists. Sometimes they also perform investigations in the air or on land.

## Security Guard

Security guards protect people against many dangerous threats. These include fire, theft, and terrorism. They must stay alert and watch for any suspicious activity. They may patrol an area or use security cameras to make sure everything is safe.

## Secret Service Agent

A secret service agent protects high government officials and their families. These include the president, the vice-president, former presidents, and visiting dignitaries. The position often involves investigations. Agents also keep close watch on possible criminals. They do undercover work, too.

# Glossary

**ammunition**
Bullets, bombs, or anything that can be shot from a gun or exploded as a weapon.

**Bronze Star**
A medal awarded to a member of the military for heroism during a conflict.

**detonate**
To make a bomb explode.

**discrimination**
The unjust treatment of someone because of their gender.

**fuse**
The part of a bomb that once it is lit makes the bomb explode after a certain length of time.

**hazardous**
Dangerous or risky.

**psychological**
Something that affects the mind or the way someone thinks.

**ordnance**
The part of the military dealing with the supply and storage of weapons and combat vehicles.

**remote**
Far away.

**terrorist**
A person who uses violence and fear against regular citizens for a political reason.

**trainee**
Someone who is learning how to do a certain job or profession.

**ventilation**
Something that brings in fresh air.

# Read More

Baxter, Roberta. *Bomb Squad Technicians in Action (Dangerous Jobs in Action)*. North Mankato, MN: The Child's World, 2017.

Fitzgerald, Lee. *Bomb Squads (Careers for Heroes)*. New York, NY: PowerKids Press, 2016.

Petersen, Justin. *Bomb Disposal Units: Disarming Deadly Explosives*. North Mankato, MN: Capstone Press, 2016.

## Visit 12StoryLibrary.com

Scan the code or use your school's login at **12StoryLibrary.com** for recent updates about this topic and a full digital version of this book. Enjoy free access to:

- Digital ebook
- Breaking news updates
- Live content feeds
- Videos, interactive maps, and graphics
- Additional web resources

**Note to educators:** Visit 12StoryLibrary.com/register to sign up for free premium website access. Enjoy live content plus a full digital version of every 12-Story Library book you own for every student at your school.

# Index

## About the Author

Samantha S. Bell has written more than 125 nonfiction books for children. She also teaches art and creative writing to children and adults. She lives in the Carolinas with her family and too many cats.

**READ MORE FROM 12-STORY LIBRARY**

Every 12-Story Library Book is available in many formats. For more information, visit **12StoryLibrary.com**